4 GODLY TOOLS
for a Happy Marriage

4 GODLY TOOLS
for a Happy Marriage

JOHN SHARROCK

XULON PRESS

Xulon Press
2301 Lucien Way #415
Maitland, FL 32751
407.339.4217
www.xulonpress.com

© 2020 by John Sharrock

All rights reserved solely by the author. The author guarantees all contents are original and do not infringe upon the legal rights of any other person or work. No part of this book may be reproduced in any form without the permission of the author. The views expressed in this book are not necessarily those of the publisher.

Unless otherwise indicated, Scripture quotations taken from the Holy Bible, New International Version (NIV). Copyright © 1973, 1978, 1984, 2011 by Biblica, Inc.™. Used by permission. All rights reserved.

Scripture quotations taken from the New King James Version (NKJV). Copyright © 1982 by Thomas Nelson, Inc. Used by permission. All rights reserved.

Scripture quotations taken from the New American Standard Bible (NASB). Copyright © 1960, 1962, 1963, 1968, 1971, 1972, 1973, 1975, 1977, 1995 by The Lockman Foundation. Used by permission. All rights reserved.

Paperback ISBN-13: 978-1-6322-1188-0
Ebook ISBN-13: 978-1-6322-1189-7

DEDICATION

This book is dedicated to all those that desire to have a happy marriage, one that reflects the type of relationship that the Lord God Himself wants us to have.

TABLE OF CONTENTS

Dedication...v
Acknowledgments...ix
Foreword..xi
Introduction: Why write this book? xiii

Chapter 1
Understanding the Problem:
It affects every aspect of our marriage 1

Chapter 2
Tool # 1: Live Forgiveness - the barrier destroyer.................7

Chapter 3
Tool # 2: Care for Each Other's Hearts – by changing 3 things 17

Chapter 4
Care for Each Other's Hearts by Our Words 25

Chapter 5
Care for Each Other's Hearts by Our Actions.....................33

Chapter 6
Care for Each Other's Hearts by Helping to Heal Old Wounds......41

Chapter 7
Tool # 3: Give Grace – Let Them Be Themself 47

Chapter 8
Tool # 4: Keep A Clear Account – No Past Offenses...............59

Chapter 9
Summary of What We Learned.....................................69

Appendix A 75
Bibliography..77

ACKNOWLEDGMENTS

I would like to first thank my Lord Jesus Christ, who saved me, and showed me a better way to live in a marriage than I had ever seen or experienced. My biggest encourager in this endeavor has been my wife, Anita. Without her incredible love and support, and her desire to have a Godly, happy marriage, I would not be able to express these concepts with any kind of authority, as they would only be an untested hypothesis. Without her nightly reading through the newest portion of the manuscript, it would not have been as clearly stated. I would also like to express my gratitude for the amazing contributions of Dr. Cherree Morgan and Van Savell, whose encouraging words kept me moving towards completion, and whose editing prowess significantly clarified the message.

FOREWORD

When I first read this manuscript it was like a doctoral dissertation, difficult to read and assimilate, but it's truths resonated deep within my soul. The author had a story to tell. He had broken all the rules and then discovered one by one ways to straighten out his life.

The message was **Marriage** – the "how to" learned out of the crucible of "how not to." I asked the author for a rewrite, then a second, and a third. Ultimately the manuscript went from a seldom to be read library book to a married couple's guide to happiness and success.

Now I can't wait to walk through word for word the transformational message in John Sharrock's book. I still have lots to learn, and I have been married 57 years.

Van Savell

Introduction

WHY WRITE THIS BOOK?

Marriage is hard work. We experience difficult times interacting with our spouse. Things ranging from a simple misunderstanding to a betrayal. The latter cuts to our very core. Unresolved negative emotions, like anger or embarrassment, lead to emotional wounds. We tend to bury them, creating walls around our heart. When we do so we hope they will go away. However, the ugly truth is: the pain resurfaces, usually as an angry outburst. And these walls only separate us from our spouse.

Books about fixing our marriage relationship are everywhere. We can find them in the check-out line at the grocery store, in airport gift shops, drug stores and discount dollar stores. Entire sections of websites, bookstores and libraries are dedicated to the latest and greatest ways to fix our marriage relationship. We can even read a series of articles over several months' worth of magazines. Few have godly solutions.

As we look around today's world, we see marriage in disarray. Families are falling apart. Husbands and wives hurt each other emotionally. The person hurt lashes out in response, creating more hurts. They spiral downward, blaming each other, getting angrier, then try to kiss and make up. Seldom is there resolution.

The marriage success rate is in a downward decline, not just in society in general, but even within the church community. This epidemic is indicative of our failure to learn a better way to live with our spouses. Our mistakes and the mistakes of our parents are passed down to our children.

Healthy marriages are foundational to any continuing society. It all began in the Garden of Eden, where God created Eve to be the match for Adam. A healthy marriage is one where a mutual adoration and caring for each other's hearts is a way of life. It is a relationship where the husband loves his wife, "as Christ loved the church and gave his life for her," Paul tells us in Ephesians 5:25 (NKJV 2007). It is also where the wife respects her husband. Paul makes it clear in verse 33 where he wrote: "Nevertheless, let each one of you in particular so love his own wife as himself, and let the wife see that she respects her husband."

So why am I writing a book and adding to the seemingly endless noise of "fix your relationship here" titles? What makes me think I can help you enjoy your marriage for the rest of your life? Let me tell you a little about myself.

Born in Ohio, I was raised in Virginia, and moved to Louisiana permanently upon my arrival at LSU in January 1980. My family of origin taught me I was the scapegoat for almost anything that happened. I learned being manipulated or punished was the proper treatment for me. I learned to survive by developing coping actions. I then married a woman raised in a differently dysfunctional family. I had proposed marriage about eight weeks after meeting her.

Unfortunately, we had little or no emotional intimacy after our wedding. By our third anniversary, our patterns of hurting each other were well established. Proper resolution was never

Why Write This Book?

achieved. There was no grace given. There was little caring for each other's hearts by words or actions. There was no help in healing wounds. At times forgiveness was sought or given. Yes, there were occasions caring for each other's hearts occurred. These were few, and far between. Ultimately, a mindset evolved of "Why try; I'll just be rejected." Once established, it was hopeless to try to repair our marriage.

After the death of that marriage, God orchestrated my second. Anita and I have mental and emotional intimacy. It continues to get deeper. Don't get me wrong, we have our bad days, even weeks. But there is a difference in how we treat each other. We work together to resolve hurts or understand each other's thoughts or motives. Are we perfect at giving forgiveness or keeping a clear account? How about giving grace or caring for each other's hearts? No, we aren't. We aren't perfect.

After more than seven years together, and more than 6 years of marriage, we are more in love with each other now than we were then. Our joy and contentment with our marriage relationship continue to increase. The results speak for themselves. I can tell you from personal experience, God's principles work — always. Ignored, they don't!

Back to my question: Why me as an author on this subject? Because, as I look back on a broken and failed first marriage while experiencing the joy of a fruitful second marriage, I see the differences. The same is true when I consider my parents relationship, and the times I spent observing my first wife's parents. Thinking about those earlier relationships, it is obvious how those relational failures created coping habits. My first wife and I then repeated our failures, repeated our coping habits and continued hurting each other. The repetition ended up destroying that marriage.

What were those failures? We did not follow God's relationship instructions.

Through great emotional pain and by the leading of the Holy Spirit, I have learned biblical life-changing concepts that enable us to fix our relational failures. My current wife, Anita, and I have learned to heal the hurts caused by our current failures, as well as the root event that created the coping habits. We have learned we don't need to repeat those failures or habits. Nor do we need to continue to feel our old hurts. We have a choice to make. We can either continue to be a slave to our history with its negative emotions and the patterned knee-jerk responses they promote, or we can overcome those emotions and responses by following God's instructions.

This book explains those concepts. Practicing them will enable us to live together in a new level of intimacy and admiration. I say "concepts" instead of "methods" because it is impossible to give detailed step-by-step instructions. Since each person is unique and has their own way of talking, thinking and hearing, the way each concept is worked out will look different for each couple.

These concepts are the ones Anita and I diligently incorporate into our everyday interaction. My first wife and I were unable to incorporate these, because either we didn't try, or we didn't know how. In my second marriage these simple concepts have proven to keep our emotional and intimacy level high. Several years into our marriage, we are more in love with each other. That isn't just me saying it: People who have witnessed our relationship blossom say the same thing. People who knew one of us from our first marriages and hadn't seen us in years say they cannot believe the difference!

These concepts work, not because they have been proven in our relationship, but because they follow simple scriptural instructions. One major secret to success in any endeavor is to do something that is simple and repeatable. Golfers call it

"muscle memory." When we follow and repeat God's simple instructions, we can be sure we will succeed because:
God's instructions always work.
Because the concepts are simple, they are easy to duplicate. Anyone can use them. Anyone can get better at following them. If you try to follow them in your own strength and resolve, you will have some success. You may even have a decently fulfilling marriage.

If Jesus Christ is the center of your relationship, there are several things that will be more in your favor. You will have God's guidance to avoid or disarm the emotional minefields. You will gain strength to overcome obstacles. Consistently following God's instructions, with His guidance and strength, produces endurance and sustained success.

As you read the situational examples, you may recognize yourself or your spouse. You may even think I have been watching over your shoulder! I promise – I haven't! All of us have experienced similar situations. Solomon wrote about the general commonality of experience in Ecclesiastes 1:9 (NKJV 2007), "That which has been is what will be, that which is done is what will be done and there is nothing new under the sun." While some of the situational examples may be actual historical events, any names and some details have been changed to protect identities.

How do I know so well your hurtful responses that it appears I am listening to your thoughts? The same reason: I have had similar thoughts. Paul tells us in 1 Corinthians 10:13a (NKJV 2007) "No temptation has overtaken you except such as is common to man;" so you are not alone in having to work through these issues. While the details of your experience will be different from mine, the processes and wounds are the same. The instructions are the same. These how-to-fix-it concepts aren't new either, as they are written about in the New Testament and are referred to in Proverbs.

Having healthy marriages is a worthy goal and aspiration, and I know you can have even more joy, happiness and intimacy than you have ever known. My prayer is each of you will learn how to live in a marriage that others desire to emulate.

Let's begin by looking at a couple of situations illustrating some of the underlying issues we all face, and some of the schemes the enemy uses to keep us a slave to our negative emotions and responses.

1

Understanding The Problem

IT AFFECTS EVERY ASPECT OF OUR MARRIAGE

One of our greatest gifts is the ability to have deep, abiding love and friendships that last a lifetime. People meet in elementary school and become life-long best friends. Junior high students become friends, fall in love, get married and stay together until death. Both are rare and precious. Maintaining deep platonic friendships is difficult. Keeping the flames of love burning in "a one woman with one man for a lifetime marriage" can sometimes feel like mission impossible.

The enemy of God and mankind (Satan) hates successful marriages. Why? Because they illustrate the intimacy God desires to have with us as individuals. Therefore, one of the enemy's main goals is to break marriages up. He will use any and all tactics at his disposal.

Anything we do or say can be used by the enemy to hurt us or separate us from our spouse. This creates an atmosphere of wariness and self-protection. Anything done to try to fix the issue can be fuel for more wounds and separation–a vicious cycle that can take us spiraling down to bitterness and resentment.

There is hope we don't need to live in bitterness or resentment. I assure you real peace is attainable. Too often we simply try to sweep our issues under the rug. Unfortunately, instead of healing, the hurt just festers. If we add misconceptions about what our spouse is thinking or feeling, damage to our relationship in epic proportions can occur in a split second.

For instance, let's say a single man begins to frequent a strip club, and a few months later meets a wonderful girl. The new couple visit the club a few times together. Soon they agree that clubbing is not good for their relationship, so they stop. A couple of years later, the now happily married couple is going on a trip. They stop to get fuel at a truck stop on their way out of town. While he pumps the fuel, he looks around, wanting to be fully aware of his surroundings. His gaze stops at the club's sign. Recognizing the foolishness of wasting his time and money, he smiles slightly and shakes his head. She was watching him. Because he did not say what he was thinking, she made some wrong assumptions. She concluded he was wishing he could return to the "freedom" he had before they met.

Now she is offended, because she thinks he regrets being with her. A complete misunderstanding occurs, based on what she *thought* he was thinking. She prepares herself for a battle she fears is happening again. Her first husband cheated on her repeatedly. Instead of inquiring about what her current husband was thinking, she dwells on his expressions and her own conclusions, seen through the filter of her own history. Hours later, when they get to the privacy of their hotel room, he comes to enjoy time with the love of his life. Instead, he is firmly rejected. She confronts him about his desire to return to being a bachelor. An argument begins, during which he hears what caused her to think what she thought.

As soon as he understands he blurts out, "You have got to be kidding me! You have got this so wrong!" Now, she's been told she is wrong for thinking the way she does! The argument gets more and more heated. No matter what he says, she thinks he is lying. No matter what she says, he thinks she isn't listening. There is no productive communication. All that is left is a deep, sorrowful loneliness, and emotional pain.

Since neither are willing to understand the other, the relationship sours, and begins to spiral out of control. A formerly happy couple is now, at best angry with each other, but unwilling to break off the relationship. At worst, they may decide this relationship just isn't worth it.

Or how about the husband picked up at work by his adoring wife. He greets her with a previously agreed upon signal that it has been a bad day: "I need about ten minutes to decompress". She has greeted him with a sunny "Hello, honey, how was your afternoon," and he has replied with "leave me alone, I need to chill."

They drive away quietly, until she breaks the silence to inform him they are going to her best friends' house, because she left her purse over there. Since she broke the silence, he responds with a curtly worded statement. His clipped, emphatic enunciation of every syllable clearly expresses his displeasure at the silence being broken.

She's being told she needs to respect the silence her husband demanded from her, and she becomes offended. He doesn't see he is doing anything wrong, because all he asked for was silence.

After a moment, he starts to vent about the day, but then the situation escalates. He airs out his frustrations with her driving. And she asks, "Did you take it out on any customers or co-workers, or am I getting it all?" She has just added gasoline to the fire, and he verbally explodes at her.

Our first example is filled with conclusions and assumptions, based on her history with other men. She has projected offenses of the former husband onto her current husband. She prepares to fight the same fight with her innocent current husband that she had fought repeatedly with her former husband. Wrong assumptions made caused a blow-up that could have been avoided by extending grace to her husband. At least until she could understand why he had that peculiar expression on his face.

Our second example involves his history in a way she doesn't know about. He is acting out of the emotional baggage from similar events at two very good jobs he lost.

We could write an encyclopedia of examples of causes of arguments. These two examples illustrate what may be the most frequent wound-causing type of interactions.

Assuming or concluding based on our own personal history.

Your personal history is your personal history. No-one else has experienced the exact same events, nor heard the exact same words. It is impossible for any other human being in history to have the exact same thoughts of, feelings about, or reactions to a situation. It is a physical, emotional, mental and spiritual impossibility. You are unique. That unique experience factor affects the way we think about events, and creates the assumptions we make or conclusions we draw from what we see or hear. In other words, our experiences create filters that new comments and events pass through. Those filters shape how we react.

These are just a couple of examples, and there are thousands upon thousands, with all kinds of intimate details only you will know about. Every time we have been hurt it came in an instant. The wound was created through a flippant comment, a gesture or funny face at the wrong time. A wound could even happen when we have unfulfilled expectations. Whether or not what we expected was even promised.

So how do we deal with these hurts? How do we keep our relationships working positively? We will discuss four concepts that provide a foundation for healing those hurts and restoring the relationship. They will help you remove the emotional walls of separation. They will help prevent future hurtful events from taking root in your heart. As you walk out the concepts that will follow in the next few chapters, you will experience the joy of a relationship that many dream of, and few attain.

2

Tool # 1: Live Forgiveness

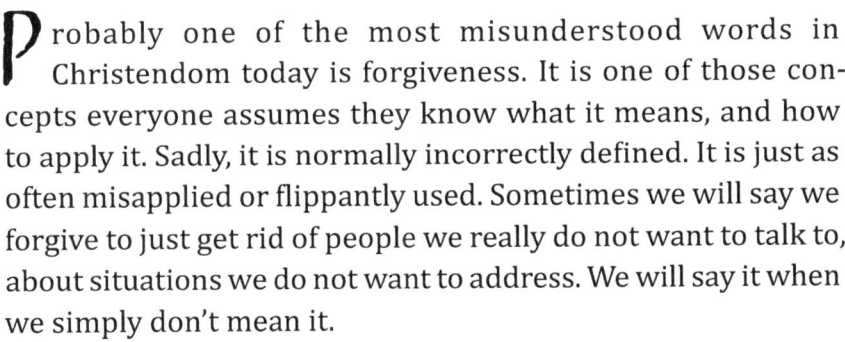

THE BARRIER DESTROYER

Probably one of the most misunderstood words in Christendom today is forgiveness. It is one of those concepts everyone assumes they know what it means, and how to apply it. Sadly, it is normally incorrectly defined. It is just as often misapplied or flippantly used. Sometimes we will say we forgive to just get rid of people we really do not want to talk to, about situations we do not want to address. We will say it when we simply don't mean it.

When forgiveness is correctly understood and properly used, it's power to change our lives is incredible! It allows us to

- receive healing for those hurts we have been given
- disarm the trigger that causes senseless emotional reactions
- remove protective emotional walls around our hearts
- have reconciliation and restoration of the relationship

When you hear someone talking about forgiveness, what comes to your mind? Most people think about letting go, or letting bygones be bygones, or letting it be 'water under the bridge', or some other kind of "push it out of our mind and sight" concept. Many think forgiveness requires them to turn the other cheek and allow the person who offended them to continue doing what they did, without any change in their behavior. Many use forgiveness to say they have accepted an apology.

However, those concepts don't even scratch the surface of forgiveness. It is so much more. Its effects are far reaching. Many of us remember what Christ has done for us at the cross. We think of the Father's righteous anger removed, and all kinds of scriptures about how He forgets our sin.

WHEN DO I FORGIVE?

While those scriptures are very true and are at the very center of our salvation, how and when are WE supposed to use it? Jesus tells us in Luke 17:4(NIV 1991) "If he sins against you seven times in a day, and seven times comes back to you and says, 'I repent', forgive him." Ladies, just so you don't think he was talking exclusively to the men, in Jesus day, Israel was a patriarchal society. Everything was accounted for and reckoned through the male line for inheritance and ownership. Teachers used the masculine pronouns and tenses of verbs. It was understood by the audience that all the teachings and standards were to apply to everyone, man, woman, or child.

Obviously, since Jesus says," if he sins... forgive him," he expects we are going to forgive. Jesus assumes forgiveness will be our normal mode of relating with others.

In Matthew 6: 9-13 (NIV 1991), after the disciples asked to be taught to pray, Christ gives us a model prayer. Then Matthew records Christ said something very instructive. "If you forgive men when they sin against you, ..." Some critical concepts about forgiveness are stated here by Christ. Understanding them will give us a better comprehension of how pervasive it should be in our lives. Keep in mind, when he is explaining the model prayer, he is talking to the disciples, which would have been the Twelve Apostles, and any other men and women who were following Christ around to hear his teaching. By extension of instructing all the believers of his day, he is also talking directly to us.

First, he says "If you forgive your brother". "If" is a seemingly innocuous word, yet it carries a very powerful message! "If you forgive." We can choose to forgive or to not forgive. It is so important that we grasp the concept here, I will say it again.

We have the ability to choose to forgive, or not. It is a free will choice we can make.

Then Christ says, "when he sins against you," Wow. When he sins against you. Let's look at this phrase very carefully, because the depth of truth here is incredible. Whenever the word "when" is used as a conjunctive adverb, it can refer to a very specific time period normally defined by the next few words in the phrase. Since the rest of the phrase says, "he sins against you", one meaning is whenever the sin occurs, we should forgive. The time frame when forgiveness should be given is immediate. Literally, while the event is occurring.

The word "when" can also be used as a warning that certain actions or events are going to occur. We should expect to be sinned against. And we should be prepared to forgive.

HOW OFTEN SHOULD I FORGIVE?

In Matthew 18:21 (NIV 1991), Simon Peter asks Jesus, "Lord, how many times shall I forgive my brother when he sins against me? Up to seven times?" Peter was looking for an achievement standard to measure himself by. The reply Jesus makes must have amazed Peter, or any other person listening in on the conversation: *"I tell you, not seven times, but seventy seven times."* (some translations read "seventy times seven"). To us, either is just a number, and while it is a rather large one in comparison to Peter's, it is still a measurable standard. However, the way Jesus put this phrase together, a very specific concept astounded his listeners: an infinite number of times. From a personal perspective: every single time someone sins against us.

It takes more strength of character to forgive consistently and completely than we have as human beings. One reason is, when we are sinned against, we receive emotional wounds. We immediately build protective walls to prevent the wound from being seen. Those walls include early warning sensors that put us on guard when we encounter the offender. Many times the hurt is so deep, the mere mention of a person's name can bring the full range of our pain back to the forefront. And we can't get past the walls we have erected to protect ourselves. It is an emotional impossibility.

Another reason is we cannot give what we do not have. Just like if we don't have any money, we cannot provide spontaneous fun events for our family, or special treats like ice cream. If we have not received forgiveness from God, we cannot forgive others.

Now that we have a better understanding of when and how often we should forgive, we need to understand what we need to have, to be able to give it. Forgiveness is such an act of unselfishness we won't normally choose it. The forgiveness Christ is talking about is an act of free will that is not possible for us to accomplish by ourselves. We need more spiritual strength than we have as human beings. It takes the power of God working in us and through us to accomplish forgiveness.

The only way this forgiveness can be fully enacted by us is to know the author of it: Jesus Christ, and to know Him as personal Lord and Savior. Please see appendix A.

THE EFFECTS OF UNFORGIVENESS

In the Matthew passage, Christ said "if you forgive your brother...", meaning we have the option to not forgive. Allow me to give you an example of a potential long-term effect of unforgiveness. Think for a moment about someone that offended you several years ago. We'll call him Terry. Think about the event: Is your blood pressure rising? Is your heart beginning to race, or your palms getting sweaty, or do you find yourself getting angry or wanting to cry all over again? Then the hurt is unresolved. The offense is unforgiven.

Terry has been living his life since the event occurred, as have you. However, there is a huge difference in your emotional life. Terry has no baggage. Every time Terry thinks of you, he thinks of the wonderful person you are, and the fun times you have had together. Whenever Terry sees you, there is nothing to hinder his enjoyment and pleasure at seeing you. He doesn't try to duck and hide from you in the grocery store when you come around the corner of the cereal aisle.

Let's say a mutual friend (we'll call him Joe) meets you for a cup of coffee eighteen months later. Joe begins telling a story about being at a local fishing pier and reeling in what is probably about a two pound catfish, only to have the rod suddenly bend the angle usually reserved for the fight of a twenty pound trout. As he fought to keep the fish from going under the pier, Terry came running over to give a hand to land the apparent monster. At the mention of Terry's name, you immediately begin to feel anger, and disappointment. A story you have been enjoying immensely, suddenly becomes bad news that you really didn't want to hear. The reference to Terry has affected your time with Joe and destroyed the afternoon coffee. Even though you had planned to spend another hour with Joe, you make an excuse about a remembered chore or errand and cut your visit short.

Your wonderful visit with Joe was ruined by encountering Terry through his part in the fishing story. Now, whenever you see or talk with Joe, the emotions that caused you to end your coffee visit will resurface. You may not remember any of the wonderful events you share. Your great friendship with Joe has become collateral damage to the offense Terry committed against you months before, because you have not forgiven Terry.

We have looked at God's expectation for when and how often we should forgive. We have learned it is a choice we can make. We now understand there are far reaching consequences for not forgiving. Making forgiveness an integral part of everything we do, is one of the most perfect expressions of love we can give. It is a method of truly laying down our life for our friends.

FORGIVENESS DEFINED

But what is forgiveness? We discussed the most frequently given answers earlier. There are hundreds of different versions of them, and they all have a portion of what true forgiveness is all about. But none of them approach what our Heavenly Father has done for us. Since the same word is used to describe what God has done and what we are to do for our brothers, He expects us to follow in His path. None of the definitions mentioned earlier are in the same neighborhood as His actions. To live it, we need to be able to express it without using the word or any of its forms as part of the definition.

Through great emotional pain for both me and my family, God taught me what it means to forgive. I had to forgive someone who had repeatedly hurt me for several years, leaving deep emotional scars. Here is the definition I learned:

Forgiveness is:

- a will choice made and acted upon,
  - in spite of evidence or emotion to the contrary,
- to give up all our rights to
  - remain angry, hurt, or offended (fill-in your own emotional response) or
  - demand punishment, consequences, retribution, apology or explanation.

By giving up those rights, while ignoring emotions and evidence, you release the bondage you have been placed under by the enemy. Sooner or later, your emotions will follow suit.

**If you wait until your anger disappears,
or the hurt goes away before you forgive:
You will never forgive.**

Only after you forgive, can the wound be healed. As the wound is healed the emotions can disappear too.

When you forgive, the demand for punishment or consequences, retribution or apology is no longer there, because the offense has been washed away. It doesn't mean the action has been erased, as it is an historical event. The event is still there, and you may still remember it happened; however, your emotional response will not be remembered.

So is forgiveness for you, or Terry? The biggest winner is you, as you are no longer living with the weight of the emotional baggage. Just as you have access to The Father, Terry has access to spend time with you. He receives a benefit, but he doesn't need to know we forgave him. Should he come later to apologize and seek forgiveness, you can honestly tell him, "I forgave you a long time ago," or "I forgave you when it happened." You laid down your emotional life for your friend. If a friendship is made better by it, how much more will your marriage be made better by living forgiveness?

Forgiveness clears the emotional and spiritual air. It allows for the walls of protection to be destroyed. Let me give a caution: I am not talking about restoring toxic relationships of manipulation or abuse of any kind. Those types of relationships and situations are subjects requiring more than this book is designed to address.

While forgiveness is for us as the offended, there is another part of the relationship we need to be aware of, as we are taught in Philippians 2:3-4 (NIV 1991) "Do nothing out of selfish ambition or vain conceit, but in humility consider others better than yourselves. Each of you should look not only to your own interests, but also to the interests of others." If we are going to look out for the interests of our spouse, we need to be caring for each other's hearts with our words, our actions, and by helping to heal old wounds.

Summary

LIVE FORGIVENESS

Forgiveness is an act that we choose in spite of evidence or our emotions.

Forgiveness can be given as early as during the event.

If we wait until our anger or hurt goes away to forgive, we won't.

We give up all of our rights to remain angry or hurt, or to hold the offense against them.

We give up our rights for any kind of penalty or punishment to the offender.

The offender should be told forgiveness was given only when they ask for it.

3

Tool # 2: Care for Each Other's Heart

BY CHANGING 3 THINGS

Caring for each other's heart is a concept that can be difficult to understand. We will take some time to develop it. We all love the good attributes: the way our spouse shows compassion, the way they encourage, defend or support us. The way they care for our children. We can love the way they use humor. These are all good dimensions of the heart. Easy to enjoy. They are what attracts us to each other.

Caring for each other's heart encompasses every interaction. How we treat them on a minute by minute basis. How we talk to them. How we deal with the hurts our spouse is carrying from their past. How we respond to their triggered reactions.

Paul wrote about caring for each other's hearts in the marriage relationship, in Ephesians 5: 25-32. (NIV) "Husbands, love your wives, just as Christ loved the church and gave himself up for her to make her holy, cleansing her by the washing with water through the word, and to present her to himself as a radiant church, without stain or wrinkle or any other blemish, but holy and blameless.

In this same way, husbands ought to love their wives as their own bodies. He who loves his wife loves himself. After all, no one ever hated his own body, but he feeds and cares for it, just as Christ does the church – for we are members of his body. For this reason, a man will leave his father and mother and be united to his wife, and the two will become one flesh.

This is a profound mystery – but I am writing about Christ and the church. However, each one of you must also love his wife as he loves himself, and the wife must respect her husband."

I would like to focus on just a couple of the verses. We will start with the instructions for the husband.

HUSBANDS LOVE YOUR WIVES

Husbands are told to "love your wives, as Christ loved the church and gave Himself for her" in verse 25. In verse 28, husbands are told to "love their own wives as their own bodies", and in verse 33 "However, each one of you must also love his wife as he loves himself."

We should take notice of instructions given several times. Husbands loving their wives is stated repeatedly. What is not stated is also important. Paul did not write anything about providing for their needs, like food, housing and clothing. Those actions are second nature for husbands in general.

Why does Paul tell husbands to love their wives? Love is not the easiest concept for men to enact. It does not come intuitively like providing does. So, what does this love look like?

In 1 Corinthians 13: 4-8a, Paul clearly describes what love looks like:

> Love is patient.
> Love is kind.
> Love does not envy.
> Love does not boast.
> Love is not proud.
> Love does not dishonor others.

Love is not self-seeking.
Love is not easily angered.
Love keeps no record of wrongs.
Love does not delight in evil.
Love rejoices with the truth.
Love always protects.
Love always trusts, always hopes, always perseveres.
Love never fails.

This describes an unselfish love. An unconditional love. It should be expressed in every aspect of a husband's interaction with his wife. In his words, actions and attitudes. The result of that kind of love is incredible! Paul tells us how the church, the bride of Christ will look in heaven. In Ephesians 5: 27 (NIV) Paul wrote "and to present her to Himself as a radiant church without stain or wrinkle or any other blemish, but holy and blameless." Before you begin saying your wife already has wrinkles or blemishes, the church is a spiritual being, therefore we are looking at the spiritual appearance of the wife.

The reason I can say this is a description of wives is because the next verse begins "So husbands ought to love their wives..." Is she joyful and content or sad and miserable? If the wife is being loved by the husband the way Christ loved the church, then she will be joyful and content. Everyone who looks at her will see a glowing woman whose inner beauty emanates from every pore.

When the scriptures tell us about a concept, followed by the results that come from the use of it, and then instruct us to use it, the result described applies to our actions as well.

Therefore, when a husband loves his wife as Christ loved the church, she will be radiant, and beautiful and happy.

If a wife is NOT radiant, beautiful and happy, the wise man will realize something is not right, and ask her about it. The wise woman will help him resolve the situation. After the situation is resolved, her emotions will follow.

I can hear the questions now: "John, how can we have that result? Just tell me what to do! What are the steps I need to follow?" Unfortunately, there is not a one size fits all formula. The details are different, because each wife is different. But the concept is simple.

The sequence of these events is an important detail for husbands to pay attention to: Christ acts and then the church responds. He loves her unconditionally, and she becomes his radiant unblemished bride. The same is true for husbands. The scriptures are clear in the sequence. Husbands act, wives respond.

Not sure this pattern holds true in your marriage? How does she respond when you walk through the door after a bad day at the office and immediately begin to vent, and then start to complain about or fuss at her? She responds by getting defensive and meeting your emotional outburst with one of her own. Or when you come home and surprise her with a smile, gentle hug and kiss, a bouquet of her favorite flowers or reservations to her favorite restaurant, she may respond with delight.

If this is true in single events, it will become more obvious in a pattern of events that shape the path of your marriage. The evidence can be seen by all who look at both of you. Either you will be happy, or you will be miserable. It will show in your faces, especially hers.

Something not obvious until we meditate on these scriptures is the type of love shown here: unconditional love. There are no prerequisites to the wife receiving the love, because the full responsibility for the existence and her experience of that love rests with the husband. It is a love that exists separate from and prior to her responses and is shown by the way he treats her.

Look at the phrases that are written after the word "as": "as Christ loved the church and gave Himself for her," and "as their own bodies" and "as themselves." Since husbands don't put conditions on loving themselves, there should be no conditions on loving their wives. There shouldn't be any standards of behavior they need to follow. There shouldn't be any standards of appearance to be adhered to. This is unconditional love.

Every husband knows how to provide for physical needs. They are obvious: food, clothing, shelter and transportation. Many husbands do not know how to care for their wife's spiritual and emotional needs. Paul tells us in 1 Corinthians 11:3 (NIV 1991) "Now I want you to realize that the head of every man is Christ, and the head of the woman is man, and the head of Christ is God." Therefore, it is the responsibility of the husband to be the spiritual leader of the home. Caring for her Spiritual needs can be explained easily:

- pray for her and with her daily,
- read the scriptures together and discuss them daily,
- worship together on a regular basis.

Caring for her emotional needs involves so much more than hugs, or private times together. Yes, hugs and physical intimacy are vital. Infinitely more needful is showing our love by our words, our actions, and our help in healing her old wounds (More on those later!).

WIVES RESPECT YOUR HUSBANDS

In the same group of verses in Ephesians 5 where we find the instructions to the husbands to love their wives, Paul also tells wives how they should act. Just as he does not tell the husbands to provide for her physical needs, Paul does not instruct the wives to love their husbands. Instead he tells them in the NASB 95, Ephesians 5:33b," and the wife must see to it that she respects her husband."

To the Greek of Paul's day, a fuller connotation would have been understood than just respect. They would have heard: she holds him in high esteem. She acts like he is someone to be listened to for advice or direction. She trusts his thoughts and opinions more than outsiders. She considers him someone to be admired and looked up to, and depended on for leadership.

Paul tells men to love and women to respect because of two primary reasons:

Our action is our spouse's primary need from us.

Our action does not come naturally to us.

Understanding each other's needs is the beginning of caring for each other's hearts. Some practical concepts we can utilize to actively care for each other's hearts involve our words, our actions and attitudes, and helping to heal old emotional wounds. We will look at those ideas one by one through the next several chapters.

Summary

> ## CARE FOR EACH OTHER'S HEARTS

Caring for each other's hearts is acting out God's instructions for proper relationships.

Husbands loving their wives.

Wives respecting their husbands.

Thinking about our spouse instead of ourselves.

Our instructed actions are our spouses primary need from us.

4

CARE FOR EACH OTHER'S HEARTS BY OUR WORDS

There is a negative relationship behavior that is the norm in society today. It is such an accepted part of our life we will deny it is negative. We may even claim it as a sign of our great affection and respect. What is the negative behavior? Being critical or judgmental with our words.

Jesus teaches against this behavior. In Luke 6:37 (NIV 1991) we read: "Do not judge, and you will not be judged. Do not condemn, and you will not be condemned. Forgive, and you will be forgiven," While Jesus wants us to live in harmony with all our fellow human beings, in this book we will apply this to our spouses.

Judging is a consistent criticizing of imperfections. It can be about clothes, habits, or actions, just to name a few. We may even label it "constructive criticism". Those two words don't go together. Constructive builds up. Criticism tears down.

Repetitive criticizing will be internalized. Once internalization starts, all criticisms attack the self-worth of the hearer. Even when something critical is said in jest or followed up with an "I was just joking" statement. The humor will be lost on the target of the criticism. They will not feel the lightheartedness intended. They will only hear it as confirmation of their short comings.

Condemning isn't limited to a judge or jury declaring someone guilty. Condemnation is so prevalent in our society today we are considered abnormal if we don't condemn others. Sometimes we are fussed at for not eagerly accepting it. However, it is even more damaging to self-worth than criticism. Why would Jesus tell us to not condemn? Condemnation is criticism on steroids. We openly declare our spouse to be unworthy of approval. We declare ourselves to be superior.

Jesus told us to not criticize or condemn. Paul gives us an instruction about how we should change our speech. In Ephesians 4:29 NASB 95 we find: "Let no unwholesome word proceed from your mouth, but only such a word as is good for edification according to the need of the moment, so that it will give grace to those who hear."

In Greek, the word translated "unwholesome" means corrupt, rotten or worthless. No rotten words should be spoken out loud. We then read "but only such a word as is good for edification" should proceed from our mouth. Sound familiar? Does the sentence "If you can't say anything nice, don't say anything at all" come to mind? The Greek concept good incorporates benefit. Necessary edification implies furnishing the solution to the need to be built up.

Proverbs 15:4 (NKJV) gives an insight into the different results: "A wholesome tongue is a tree of life, but perverseness in it breaks the spirit." A wholesome tongue is described to the Hebrew as something they knew as sheltering, comforting and life giving. Trees are important in Hebrew thought as places of strength.

Conversely, a perverse tongue breaks the spirit. Perverseness, *'celeph" in* Hebrew, is also defined in Strong's as viciousness. The only other time this form of the word occurs in the Scripture is found in Proverbs 11:3 (NKJV), and it gives a different perspective of how destructive the perverse tongue is: "The integrity of the upright will guide them, but the perversity of the unfaithful will destroy them." The Hebrew concept translated destroy includes ravaging, like a swarm of locusts devouring a green field and stripping it bare of vegetation.

Our spoken words are very important. Proverbs 18:21 (NKJV) tells us "Death and life are in the power of the tongue, and those who love it will eat its fruit." What we say brings life or death to the spirit of the hearer.

What we say today and repeat tomorrow can influence the way someone thinks about themselves for the rest of their life.

A LIFE DESTROYED

I am reminded of a story I heard about a 25-year-old man known as Mean Matt. Mean Matt was in prison for the rest of his life because his meanness had turned violent. He had beaten a man to death with his fists. While this story is about what was spoken and reinforced early in Matt's life, the effects of our words to our spouse can be just as emotionally destructive.

None of Mean Matt's relatives were mean or violent. He acted differently from the rest of the family. Matt wasn't always mean. The events creating the nickname seemed harmless when they occurred. As his life played out, statements repeatedly made in jest became Matt's identity. When Matt was about two years old, his father's extended family had gotten together. All the young cousins were in a single room playing, with several adults watching and having a conversation around them.

Steven, one of his older cousins, had taken a toy Matt was playing with, and walked away. Matt jumped up, ran over to where his cousin was, and engaged in a tug of war for the toy. Since Steven had a stronger grip, Matt could not force him to relinquish the toy. Matt got angry, punched Steven on the arm and snarled at him. Steven gave up the toy, not wanting to receive the wrath of his younger cousin anymore. The adults in the room called him "Mean Matt", mimicked his face and snarl, and then laughed. It became a story that was told or re-enacted at every family gathering for the next several years, with everyone laughing at the "hilarious" antics of an angry toddler.

The rest of his growing up years he was called Mean Matt by his cousins. He was rewarded by the riotous laughter of the adults he adored. He became Mean Matt. His meanness turned to violence. His violence became murder. Matt's family's inadvertent words had spoken death over him.

This is an extreme case, but the point is clear: Words are important. Words can be dangerous. Words can sentence people to a miserable existence until they die. But the opposite is true also: encouraging words can give life.

A LIFE SAVED

At a graduation ceremony, the valedictorian was not giving the typical "we look to the future" speech. Steve's topic was affirming words spoken. Steve told the story of an event in his life. He was taking all his schoolbooks home. The excuse he gave? Going home to study all weekend in peace and quiet, because his family was going to be out of town. As he walked home, Steve stumbled, and dropped the books. Tom, one of the more popular athletes at school, happened to be walking home along the same route. He stopped and offered to help carry some of the books, at least as far as his own house. As they walked, they talked and laughed about events of the day. They joked about the differences between them, the popular athlete and the bookworm.

Tom invited Steve to stop for a while at his house. As it got close to supper time, Tom said he had enjoyed Steve's company, and found him to be funny. He invited Steve to eat supper with his family and to spend time with them over the weekend. A friendship was begun.

I can hear your question now. What's the big deal about that episode? Here's the rest of the story: Steve was not planning to study that weekend. He was going to commit suicide. However, because of the words spoken by Tom, he decided to postpone putting his plan into action. Because of words of affirmation spoken, a life was saved. Yes, this story is not between a husband and wife, but it shows the tongue has power to give life. A single event of affirming words changed the course of a life.

What would happen if we consistently spoke life giving words of affirmation to our spouses instead criticisms and condemnations?

WORDS SPOKEN TO OURSELVES

Not only are our spoken words life affirming or destroying, so are the words we think to ourselves. Those sneaky, snarky thought comments erode our belief in our spouse. We will not see the damage we did to our relationship until a storm hits. A part of our facade will fall off and expose the damage.

I recently had a tree cut down because I could see insects had eaten a section of the trunk, just above ground level. Most of the damage was exposed after the tree was cut down. Because the termites were eating from the ground up, the base was compromised. Had a strong enough storm arrived, the tree would have fallen over. Anything in its path would have been damaged or destroyed, including my home.

The same concept of "death and life" is true about our thoughts. If we think criticisms about our spouse, we are secretly destroying our relationship from the inside. If we think affirmations, we are edifying and strengthening our relationship.

If you wanted to grow a healthy garden, would you feed the plants poison or fertilizer? Our words are an audible method of giving mental and emotional fertilizer or poison to our spouse.

"Death and life are in the power of the tongue". Choosing your words well will help you care for each other's heart.

Equally important as our words in caring for each other's hearts are our actions towards our spouse. Our actions need to follow our words. If they do, our spouse will know our words are not just window dressing. The truth of our words and actions working together in harmony will multiply the caring for each other's hearts. Let's explore how our actions can care for each other's hearts.

Summary

> ## CARE FOR EACH OTHER'S HEARTS BY OUR WORDS

Our words affect lives for better or worse.

Critical or condemning words are emotional poison.

Affirming, encouraging or uplifting words are emotional fertilizer.

Our silent thoughts about our spouse are as important as our spoken words.

We need to increase affirmations.

We need to end criticisms and condemnations.

5

CARE FOR EACH OTHER'S HEARTS BY OUR ACTIONS

Words carry great weight and impact. Our actions do also. Little things done repeatedly become big positives or big negatives in our marriage. There are several scriptures that talk about how we should treat other people. When we apply them to our marriage, we will be caring for our spouse's heart by our actions.

In Galatians 5:22-26 (NIV 1991) Paul writes about nine positive attributes. He also gives a caution against three negative actions:

"But the fruit of the Spirit is love, joy, peace, patience, kindness, goodness, faithfulness, gentleness and self-control. Against such things there is no law.

Those who belong to Christ Jesus have crucified the sinful nature with its passions and desires. Since we live by the Spirit, let us keep in step with the Spirit.

Let us not become conceited, provoking and envying each other."

If these nine positive attributes are present in our lives, our actions will demonstrate caring for each other's hearts. Each one, taken by itself, will have positive impact in our lives. As we develop more of these attributes, the more pleasant life will become. Our relationship will become more open, transparent, intimate and satisfying.

While a study of the entire passage would be profitable, we will focus on only a couple of the traits or behaviors listed above.

In English, the word "love" has many applications and connotations. It can describe our opinions on the beauty of something we have seen, an activity we enjoy, or a food. The same word can tell the extent of our relationship feelings, sexual, sibling, friendship or romantic. In Greek there are separate words for the different types of relational love: eros, phileo, and agape. Eros is sexual attraction, phileo describes sibling love or friendship love, while agape indicates an unconditional love. A God-like love.

Eros is a desire to enjoy each other physically. Eros is conditional on our pleasure, whether our spouse receives pleasure or not. Very selfish. It can end.

Phileo is a love that can strengthen and weaken. It's strength is conditional on situations and discussions. Sometimes selfish, and sometimes selfless. It can end.

Agape is a love that always seeks the best for the other person. It does not have a list of required behaviors. Agape love exists in spite of words or actions. Agape is unconditional. It does need to be returned or even accepted. Completely selfless. Has no end.

The Greek word translated love in this passage of Galatians is agape. It is used elsewhere to describe the love God has for us. A great example is found in Ephesians 2:4 (NKJV) where Paul wrote "But God, who is rich in mercy, because of His great love with which He loved us." Agape is the root word here for both "love" and "loved". The word translated "loved" here is the exact tense we find in John 3:16 (NKJV) when the apostle John wrote "For God so loved the world that he gave his only begotten Son..." This unconditional love is in spite of the recipient's behaviors, and there is nothing the recipient can do to change it. The only options available to the recipient are to accept it or reject it.

Agape love is the type we are to have for our spouse. Unconditional.

THE THREE NEGATIVE BEHAVIORS

In Galatians 5:26 (NKJV), Paul gives us a caution against three behaviors: "Let us not become conceited, provoking and envying each other." Conceit, provocation and envy are in direct conflict with the fruits of the Spirit.

Being conceited goes directly against love and patience. Conceit is the word translated from the Greek word "*kenodoxos*", which, according to the Strong's means vain-glorious, or desirous or vain-glory, ie: self-conceited. If you are conceited, then your opinion on a subject is the only one that matters. The steps you follow to accomplish tasks are the only right way. Nobody else measures up to your standards. Anything done must be on your timetable and on your terms.

Provoking is an opposite of gentleness, kindness and peace. Provoking can be anything we say or do that creates a negative response in our spouse. The most frequent negative response is anger. We can provoke by either a conscious decision or an inadvertent action.

Envy is the last behavior Paul cautions us against here. It undermines our joy and peace. When we envy, kindness is destroyed. We act out of selfish greed. Any semblance of gentleness or self-control is lost. Wishing we have what someone else has is a desire that creates all kinds of opportunities to give hurts. It can occur in specific situations, or it can become all consuming. Either way, it is emotional poison for any relationship, especially a marriage.

In 1 Corinthians 13: 4-8, Paul gives a thorough description of unconditional love. It is very challenging (see listing in the chapter 3 Care for Each Other's Heart)! What a high standard for both behavior and attitude! We can attain to it, or else God wouldn't have had Paul write it.

Paul cautions us against a series of attitudes and behaviors that are not a part of love: envy, conceit, selfishness, anger, and thinking evil. Consistently saying "no" to those attitudes or behaviors is not possible in our own strength. Yet, Philippians 4:13 (NKJV) tells us, we can do all things through Christ who strengthens us. Meaning, we already have the ability and strength to live without negative behaviors.

Many of us think about our spouses actions a great deal, trying to figure out their motives and reasons. It is easy to assign negative motives or reasons based on our own history and filters. The enemy uses our filters to distort our thinking about our spouse's words or actions. Paul tells us love "thinks no evil". Assigning negative reasons or motives is one form of thinking evil.

Thinking evil can also apply to unmet expectations. For instance, lack of doing things together becomes "I am not important anymore." Lack of private one-on-one time can be changed to "He/She doesn't want me anymore." Thinking evil by assigning negative motives or actions is a form of condemning or judging.

POSITIVE ACTIONS

There are two concepts written twice within 1 Corinthians 13 verse 8. Repetition in the scriptures is extremely important! God really wants us to grasp these ideas: "bears all things, believes all things, hopes all things, endures all things." There are two actions, and two thought patterns expressed here. Bears all things and endures all things go together as actions. Believes all things and hopes all things go together as thought patterns or attitudes.

The word translated "bears" is the Greek word "stego". According to the Strong's Concordance, it means to cover with silence, to endure patiently. The connotation is to not gossip about it. It can be translated as "bear" or "suffer". "Endures" is the Greek word "hupomeno" which means to "stay under(behind), i.e. remain." All failures against us are to be endured patiently. We are to remain in the relationship through thick and thin, without complaining about it to others. Wow! Convicting words.

Let me give a caution here, because of the context of the chapter and letter Paul wrote to the church in Corinth, abuse is not addressed. Nor is this book designed to address it either.

As I discussed this section with a pastor friend, he told me there are two words that teach us about living in a healthy relationship. Forgiveness and forbearance. Forgiveness is about dealing with being sinned against or emotionally wounded. Forbearance is about giving grace for the little idiosyncrasies that can be irritating, but don't cause a wound.

POSITIVE ATTITUDES

Let's examine the middle phrases: "believes all things, hopes all things." What a powerful group of words! The word translated here as "believes," means to have total trust and faith in. It is the same Greek word used by Luke in Acts 16:31a (NKJV) when he said, "Believe on the Lord Jesus and you shall be saved." There is no doubt in our trust in Christ, there should be no doubt in our trust of our spouse. I can hear the comments now: "John, my spouse repeatedly fails me. Jesus never will." That is true. We should still trust their taking care of us. We should still believe the best of them and the best from them. Even when they fail or hurt us. That is one reason we need to forgive.

"Hopes" has a similar meaning of expecting the best, because the same Greek word is used in Hebrews 11:1 (NKJV) to describe our faith in God himself, "Now faith is the substance of things hoped for, the evidence of things not seen."

These actions and attitudes will not happen overnight. We must decide to cultivate them. Becoming good at anything takes time and practice. A basketball player becomes great by practicing specific shots again and again, doing the appropriate passing, dribbling or rebounding drills. A quarterback becomes great by practicing his passing skills with his receivers and studying game film of his opponents. A guitar player becomes great by practicing putting their fingers in the right places and different patterns of strumming. Golfers call it muscle memory. The same concept is true about relational behaviors. We become good at something by repeating proper behaviors and by reinforcing proper thoughts in our mind.

If we want to be good at hoping, bearing and believing, we need to practice it in our thoughts. When we practice it in our thoughts, our speech, actions and emotions will change. Romans 12:2 (NKJV) tells us "And do not be conformed to this world, but be transformed by the renewing of your mind, that you may prove what is that good and acceptable and perfect will of God." If we are transformed by the renewing of our minds, we will be able to act or respond by displaying the nine different attributes of the fruit of the Spirit. When that begins to happen, we will be caring for each other's hearts by our actions.

There will be times our spouse will respond in a manner more vehement than would normally be expected from the situation. We may have hit an old un-healed wound. Helping our spouse get those wounds healed is another way of for us to care for each other's heart. In the next chapter, we will look at a few examples of helping our spouse's old wounds to be healed.

Summary

> **CARE FOR EACH OTHER'S HEARTS BY OUR ACTIONS**

If we say positive, encouraging things, our repeated actions should reinforce our words.

Simple actions can mean a lot.

Changing from a negative to a positive pattern of behavior in specific areas shows we do care about our spouses needs and desires.

Our actions need to match our words, or our words are empty.

6

CARE FOR EACH OTHER'S HEARTS BY HELPING HEAL OLD WOUNDS

We all have emotional triggers from past wounds. They can set off incredible explosions. Seemingly inconsequential events can cause a hidden emotional trigger to be activated. Most times, people who weren't involved in creating the trigger unknowingly receive the emotional consequences. How we handle those out-of-the- ordinary negative reactions is key to disarming the emotional triggers and beginning the healing process.

There are three options to handling these explosions:

1. We can do nothing and allow the explosions to continue.
2. We can react negatively and escalate the situation.
3. We can identify and work towards disarming the emotional triggers and healing the old wounds.

Is there something we can do right away to settle our spouse down? How can we set the table for resolving the issue in our spouse's heart? Admit your responsibility in the current episode. Ask forgiveness for your actions or words. The remaining details of the wounds and scenarios will differ from person to person and situation to situation. While they will be different, the concepts leading to healing are the same.

Emotional triggers can be activated by physical activity, or by our spoken words. Let's look at an example of dealing with each type of emotional trigger activation.

PHYSICALLY ACTIVATED

George and Stephanie had been dating a couple of weeks. One day, as he started tickling her, he found the spot that made her laugh hysterically, and lose the ability to fight back. He wanted to keep her at his playful mercy for as long as possible. He let up slightly for a couple of seconds, then dove back in with renewed vigor. Just after he began tickling "that place" again, Stephanie balled up into a fetal position, her knees tucked under her chin, her legs pulled tightly to her chest. She began to pant and was covered in the foul-smelling sweat of terror.

What happened here? It's just a tickle match, right? Why would Stephanie react in fear to his tickling? Those questions can only be answered after she calms down, but how does George handle the situation at hand?

There are basically two ways he can respond: in defense of himself, or towards resolution and healing. If George reacts with a negative emotion or attitude, nothing will be permanently resolved. Sure, she will eventually calm down, and they can even agree that "spot" is off limits. The immediate scenario will appear to be resolved. However, that does nothing to resolve the cause of the response. If only the immediate scenario is addressed, they will hit the same trigger in the future. Unfortunately, in a more emotionally painful way.

If George responds with a loving, unselfish attitude, both the immediate situation and the old emotional wound can be resolved to promote permanent healing.

So what should George do? Because Stephanie's emotional make-up and wound is unique, I can't tell you in the specific actions George should take or any specific words he should use, but I can give you the concepts of what should happen.

The goal is a permanent healing of the wound and disarming of the emotional trigger. In this type of situation there are five concerns:

- calm the immediate response,
- resolve any wound just given,
- identify the emotional trigger,
- identify the historical event that created the trigger
- give forgiveness for the original event, as discussed in Live Forgiveness

The immediate threat must be removed. In this example George could create a safe physical space, most likely by either completely breaking off physical contact for a moment, or by moving his hand away from the "spot". He could speak in a calm voice, using words that convey to Stephanie the threat has been terminated. Once Stephanie's negative response has subsided, George and Stephanie should talk about what occurred.

Whatever Stephanie says, George should listen without judgment or condemnation. Remain calm, talking in a low, reassuring voice. This safe atmosphere will allow Stephanie to be honest about what happened. Talking through the event in sequence will allow the trigger point to be exposed. Once the trigger point has been identified, the original wound can be exposed and healed.

Asking leading questions about similar events in her past will usually bring the emotionally remembered event back to her conscious mind. In this case, Stephanie remembered being tickled by her Dad, when she was very young. Dad kept her at his mercy, pinning her arms at her side so she could not fight back, rendering her totally helpless. What frequently happens when a young girl loses control of her body because of laughter? She urinates on herself. Since they were wrestling on Mom & Dad's bed, Dad reacted by severely punishing Stephanie.

Because the original wound has been identified, Stephanie can forgive her Dad and her heart can begin to heal. George and Stephanie can, in time, enjoy those games again, without restrictions.

VERBALLY ACTIVATED

Emotional triggers don't need to be physically activated, they can be set off by words too. David is sitting on Joe's back patio, drinking coffee and chatting. During one of the stories, David doesn't realize Joe is "pulling his leg". Joe realizes David totally missed the point and explains the story to David.

They both laugh after the explanation, until Joe laughingly says: "You are slower than I thought". To Joe, it is a flippant comment. To David it is a deep emotional cutting. The entire drive home David ponders the "slower than I thought" comment, and really begins to get down on himself. What Joe doesn't know is David's daily conversations with his parents were laced with similar critical comments.

When David arrives home, he gives his wife Nicole a quick peck on the cheek, and a single arm around the shoulder split second hug, instead of sharing the normal warm hug and gentle, loving kiss. Nicole is hurt because he is greeting her the way he says hello to her sister. She doesn't know what she has done to deserve such treatment by David. He is unaware that he is acting cold towards Nicole. He is responding to her through the filters placed over his emotions by the belittling comments of his past. David's actions are a continuation of his negative emotions from Joe's flippant comment.

In situations where historical wounds are re-opened, the order of resolution doesn't matter. What matters is that every wound receives healing. In our example, these wounds need to be resolved:

1. The rift created between Nicole and David by his apparent coldness to her
    a. Nicole will need to forgive David
    b. They may want to discuss the situation, so he can transform his greeting when he is hurting, or she can understand and give grace for his actions.
2. The wounds caused by Joe's comments
    a. David will need to forgive Joe
    b. Joe may never know of the hurt he caused, nor the forgiveness given.
3. The original wounds caused by David's parents.
    a. David will need to forgive his parents.
    b. His parents may never know of the hurts they caused, nor the forgiveness given.

    A simple method to make sure all the offenses are handled properly would be newest to oldest. Resolving the situation in the order of newest offense first prevents resentment build up from the new wound. It makes dealing with the older offenses easier, because of the momentum created by the healing that has already happened. Please be aware, there may be times where counseling may be required to assist in the healing process.

    We have all heard about the Golden Rule: Do to others as you want them to do to you. If we don't like being interrupted in our conversations, we shouldn't interrupt other people. If we don't like being manipulated, don't manipulate others. Instead: give grace.

SUMMARY

CARE FOR EACH OTHER'S HEART BY HEALING OLD WOUNDS

Emotional wounds can cause "over the top" negative reactions to current events.

We can respond to make the situation worse, or to heal the wound.

To resolve the wound we need to:

Resolve the immediate situation by forgiving.

Gently search for the root event that caused the initial wound.

Forgive the original offense.

7

Tool # 3: Give Grace

LET THEM BE THEMSELF

Giving grace is an unnatural concept of selfless behavior. A simple way to explain giving grace is letting others have the liberty to think or act different than you do. From a different perspective: treating them as you would want to be treated. Matthew 7:12 (NIV) says: "So in everything, do to others what you would have them do to you, for this sums up the Law and the Prophets." Every aspect of our marriage relationships will be better if we employ this concept.

To help us understand the depth and breadth of this instruction, I want to look at some issues that make this instruction difficult to follow. No other person in history has heard or experienced exactly what you have. Because of those historical events, emotional or mental filters are developed. In the everyday world, we understand filters to be tools to remove contaminants, like dust from the air as it circulates through the central heating or cooling system. They clean the engine oil of our cars and make our drinking water taste better. Our mental and emotional filters do the same thing for our thoughts and reactions. However, since our mental and emotional filters are twisted and warped by our negative history, they distort accurate understanding of the current event.

Most disagreements begin because filter differences create misunderstandings. I can't tell you how many times it appeared my wife Anita and I had opposing viewpoints. Frequently we were able to determine we were saying basically the same thing, from two different perspectives. It is the "is the glass half full or half empty" dilemma.

Our mental or emotional filters are like encryption codes. Countries send information to their ambassadors or generals using an encryption code.

- A message is created.
- It is typed into an encryption device.
- The encrypted message is transmitted.
- The message is received.
- It is run through a "decryption device" to translate back to regular speech.
- The message is now read.

There is only way the message can be perfectly understood: both the sender and the receiver must use the same encryption code.

When we speak the same process occurs:

- We have a thought.
- We convert it to words. (Speakers filters applied)
- We speak the words.
- The listener hears the words.
- The listener processes the words. (Listeners filters applied)

- The listener draws conclusions or makes assumptions.

Because the filters of the speaker and listener are different, vastly different concepts can be expressed. Sometimes one of you will think you are presenting something extremely clearly. Your spouse will hear, and may jump to an erroneous conclusion. We need to realize, after events or statements have gone through mental or emotional filters, the understanding obtained may not be accurate. Actions by our spouse can catch us by surprise. We may question their motives or intentions. Running those questions about motives through our filters can send us in a direction that isn't even on their radar. We have decoded their message incorrectly. When that happens, strife and discord follow.

Brandon was on vacation and was starting his day. Bill was coming over to work on a project, so Brandon suggested to his wife, Ginny, to get donuts and kolaches for breakfast. Ginny replied, "I really don't want a kolache." Brandon knew she enjoyed that breakfast as a treat, but here she is, rejecting his suggestion of it. His response was to cancel the whole idea. To his mind, she rejected all aspects of the suggestion. To her mind, she only rejected the kolache, but was accepting of the donut. A few moments later, she asked why he hadn't left to get donuts. "You don't want any. That's why." Then they have a more animated discussion about what she meant, and what he heard. Ginny said what she didn't want, thinking she had clearly indicated she was only rejecting part of his suggestion. Not all of it.

To his mind, she had clearly indicated her lack of desire for either item for breakfast. Two sets of filters receiving the same information, but not producing the same answer.

Allowing our spouse to think, speak or act differently than we do is one way to give grace.

Another way we can give grace is an ongoing process:

1. Learn how their filters are different from ours.
2. Change our "encoding filters" to match their "decoding filters".
3. Change our "decoding filters" to match their "encoding filters".

This process will not happen overnight. It will take effort by both to learn how the other thinks.

ACTIONS OR MOTIVES

Steve and Betsy were packing the car to go to their favorite fishing spot. They decided to get some Sudoku puzzle books to take with them. As they got close to the store, Steve realized it was close to lunch time, and spontaneously suggested they stop and get Betsy's favorite deli meal. While ordering, Steve remembered the deli owner, Samantha, had invited everyone in Steve's office to come visit. As he payed the bill, he asked the cashier to tell Samantha he had stopped by.

The next day, Betsy spoke to him about the scenario, "Why did you ask him to say hello for you? That just seems kind of personal to me." Steve knew her history, that her ex-husband cheated on her and lied about it. He reacted harshly to Betsy's comment, assuming she was accusing him of being like her ex, vehemently defending his action instead of explaining his thoughts. Steve's thoughts at the deli were about the business relationship. Steve thought Betsy had concluded he was trying to get personal with the owner. Betsy was only asking for understanding. The thought that Steve might be cheating never entered her mind. Nor was there emotional concern.

By being harsh and defensive, there was no grace given by Steve. He did not treat Betsy the way he would want to be treated. An example of Steve giving grace would be his not becoming defensive. He could explain his reason, that he was letting the owner know that he had accepted her general, office-wide invitation to visit her deli.

Betsy wasn't provoked by her past to ask questions. Her motive was simple curiosity. Different wording by Betsy may have allowed Steve to hear the grace Betsy was trying to give.

HELP ME UNDERSTAND

Anita and I used to ask each other, like Betsy did, "why did you say that" or "why do you think that?" We found being asked those questions put us on the defensive. Because of our filters, our minds and hearts would be on guard for an assault that history has shown is getting ready to occur. We hurriedly build walls of protection. Look out! Here comes an argument! Prepare to defend yourself!

We realized a less confrontational way to ask for clarification was needed. A great phrase she and I use frequently to bypass those filters is "help me understand."

Asking for help in understanding tells our spouse there is validity in their actions, feelings or words. It implies our understanding may need correcting, and they are the only person that can help us grasp the true meaning. The "help me understand" approach gives the opportunity to explain those actions thoughts or feelings. Defending is all but eliminated. There is no confrontation. It promotes "us".

Being non-confrontational helps you to become a team. As you become a team in the episode, there can be a feeling of victory. Other feelings can occur, but maybe the most satisfying one is the closeness and intimacy you feel, knowing you truly understand that part of your spouse's being.

Giving grace is written about in 1 Corinthians 13:4-7 (NKJV): "Love suffers long and is kind. Love does not envy; love does not parade itself, is not puffed up; does not behave rudely, does not seek its own, is not provoked, thinks no evil; does not rejoice in iniquity, but rejoices in the truth; bears all things, believes all things, hopes all things, endures all things." In the Greek, the last four phrases have deeper connotations than we understand today. I want to focus on those four phrases. Paul goes back and forth between things we don't like to deal with, and things we love to have going on: "bears all things, believes all things, hopes all things, endures all things."

Let's start our investigation of the words with a common thread through all four actions: the repeating of "all things". It literally means everything, without exception.

There are four actions that change. They are instructive about how our feelings and reactions should look. Before we delve into the actions, let me encourage you with this: God does not tell us to act in a certain way without giving us the ability and strength to accomplish it. Paul wrote in Philippians 4:13 (NKJV) "I can do all things through Christ who strengthens me." That is God's promise to us as believers.

BEARS ALL THINGS

The Greek word translated "bears" is an interesting word. The root word is used outside of scripture to describe putting a roof over a physical item. Using it to describe a relationship, "bears" means to put a covering of silence over all things. What would we need to keep silent about? The faults and errors of our spouse. We shouldn't complain about them to others. That is a tall order! Not complain? Not speak about them in a way that justifies our negative emotional responses? That's correct. We shouldn't discuss our spouse's faults and errors with others. *(Let me repeat a caution here. I am not talking about abuse of any kind. Abusive relationships require counseling this book is not able to give.)*

ENDURES ALL THINGS

As if not gossiping about it isn't enough, Paul finishes this quartet of all things descriptions with "endures". (I'll get to the two in the middle in a moment.) In Greek *"pas hupemeno"* means "all things stay behind" or "all things stay under". What does this mean: All things stay behind us and under us? That means the negative actions and words should be put behind us. We should stand over them in triumph.

BELIEVES ALL THINGS

There are two positive attitudes listed in the middle. First is believes all things. The concept a first century Greek would have understood is have faith and trust in our spouse. Faith is a reliance deeper than just lip service. It is making yourself emotionally vulnerable to your spouse. It is trusting them implicitly in all things. We should be believing for all good things to, from and for our spouse.

HOPES ALL THINGS

We have one more of the "all things" actions to look at: *"pas elpizo."* "hopes All things." We use "hope" to describe wanting something for a meal, wishing we would get a good grade on that test in school or thousands of other wants and desires. The Greek word *"elpizo"* has a much deeper connotation than the English "hope": expect or anticipate. Having an expectation our spouse is going to think the right thing, and do the right thing, and say the right thing, no matter what is happening. The Strong's Concordance shows an even deeper definition: "to anticipate, usually with pleasure". With that in mind, Paul is telling us we should be eagerly anticipating good things for and from our spouse.

These four phrases have a depth of power I have only begun to describe here. They can be applied to absolutely every area of our relationship. Because we are different people with different thought filters and emotional triggers, we are going to act, think and react different from our spouses. We will see situations differently and hear statements differently. Unfortunately, we want and expect our spouse to think and act the same way we would think or act. While identical reactions may happen on rare occasions, differing reactions are going to be the standard.

Remember, we are to cover and endure the negatives, believe and hope for the positives. We have been taught by society to assume the negative possibilities must be the truth. Not only that, we should speak them about others and must allow them to be said about us. I can assure you from personal experience, if you follow that pattern, you will develop a toxic marriage. Toxic marriages end with one of you dying from the emotional poisons, or both of you going through the bitter pain of divorce.

What would happen if we were to follow God's plan? If we endure and cover in silence the negatives. Believe in, pray for and hope for the positives. There will be more peace and less strife in our relationship. People will remark they see a dramatic change for the better.

But giving grace isn't just about our actions or words. It is also about making judgments or editorial comments. I'll never forget the look on my friend's wife's face, as she was observing her husband Terry. He was considering whether he should install the screen into the kitchen window frame, so cooler outdoor air could flow through the room. The expressions on Linda's face started with confusion. When she realized he was going to install the screen, she looked irritated, and told him "Don't do that now, I would need to move all the stuff off the windowsill, and I really don't know where to put it." He never looked in her direction, but said, "Well, if you think so." Then he let out an exasperated sigh and shook his head.

When I looked back at her, she was shaking her head, with what appeared to be a look of "What was he thinking," followed by "what is the matter with him." I asked her about her motives for saying "don't do that now." They were good, and valid. She wanted Terry to enjoy the company of their guests, instead of being busy.

Grace was not shown by Linda. She passed judgment on his actions based on what she thought was the best thing for Terry at the time. She criticized Terry's actions a couple of ways: the expressions on her face, the shaking of her head, and the tone of her voice when telling him to stop.

Before you think I am letting Terry off the hook, his sigh of resignation didn't show grace either. It was an expression of "I know better, but I will accede to your wishes." I asked him about his reasons for wanting to install the screen and open the window. He explained that the room would be more comfortable because the greater cross ventilation would make the room cooler.

Giving grace in this situation can be shown in lots of ways, I'll give a couple of examples: "Terry I am confused about what you are getting ready to do. Help me understand what you want to accomplish?" She has been non-confrontational. After explaining why he wants to install the screen, Linda can suggest that it is great he is thinking about their guests' comfort, but now might not be the best time to accomplish it, because she doesn't really want to rearrange the kitchen with guests in the house. She has allowed him the freedom to express what he wants to accomplish without judgmental comments, expressions, or sound effects. That would be Linda giving grace to Terry.

How can Terry give grace to Linda? A question Terry could ask could be: "Help me understand your reluctance for me to do this." He could then say something like: "I never thought about the other things that would need to be done, and how it would affect you for me to complete the task. I'll wait." Grace given both ways because they each believed and showed the other's thoughts and feelings about the matter were valid.

Those examples raise a question: What are we expecting from our spouse? Something good, or something harsh or hurtful? Are we eagerly anticipating their best for us, or are we preparing to protect ourselves?

Giving grace is necessary in so many aspects of our relationships, it must become an active part of our day to day relationship encounters. Giving grace would sometimes actually prevent the need to forgive, because no offense would be given, and no hurt received. If we were to consider what is being said or done considering Paul's instructions, instead of through our own filters, we wouldn't get angry as often. Many of the resulting offenses would be avoided.

Another way we can give grace is to keep a clear account, and we will look at that concept next.

Summary

GIVE GRACE

Because our histories are different, we think or respond differently.

Our filters will distort our understanding of what our spouse is saying or doing.

We should bear with and keep silent to others about the negatives of our spouse. (I am not talking about abuse here!)

We should eagerly anticipate and expect our spouse to act with our best interests in mind.

We should act with our spouses best interests in mind.

We should seek out ways to work together for understanding and resolution.

8

Tool # 4: Keep a Clear Account

NO PAST OFFENSES

We all like the intimacy we experience when we connect with someone's heart. It can be either a platonic "best-friends-forever" or a romantic relationship. It is especially wonderful when it happens in a marriage relationship. The sheer joy of not having to make sure they like you is wonderful. Even in these deep connection relationships there will be times of strife, when a wall of emotional protection is quickly erected. However, the wall erected for protection becomes much more than it was intended to be. It morphs into a wall of separation, preventing transparency and intimacy. Can we short circuit the walls? Is it possible to prevent their construction? Yes it is! Keep a clear account.

We are diligent to pay our utility bills on time. This keeps our lights on, and our water flowing. To keep our relationships flowing with intimacy, the same diligent attention is necessary. It is very easy to ignore keeping a clear account. Most of us do the opposite: we keep a scoreboard. We remember what they did or said. We think about it, fret over it. We remind ourselves of it and think we will get ours back. We will repay. This is keeping a scoreboard.

While a great teacher and his protege walked together on the seashore below the high tide mark, the teacher bent down and began writing in the sand. When he finished writing a name and event in the sand, they continued walking and turned towards the stone cliffs at the back of the beach. As they drew near to the cliffs, the teacher reached up with his hand, and ran his fingertip over some words chiseled into the rock face. As they turned to ascend the path toward the top, the disciple turned to the teacher and said: "Teacher, I don't understand. You wrote something about David in the sand, and here you have etched something in the rock about David. You quickly left the beach after writing your message in the sand, but you lingered at the rock face. What was so different about those two messages?" The wise teacher replied: "I etched his kindness to me on the cliff so I would remember it forever. I wrote of his offense against me in the sand, because the water will soon erase all evidence."

What a great illustration of keeping a clear account! I can hear your question, because I have asked it myself: "John, I get angry and say harsh things so easily. What do I do?

In Ephesians 4:26-27 (NIV) Paul writes: "In your anger do not sin; do not let the sun go down while you are still angry, and do not give the devil a foothold." Why would he say it that way? Paul presumes we will be angry at some time. He makes no excuse for it, nor does he forbid it. He simply acknowledges anger is a natural response in some situations. Then he instructs: "Do not sin."

DO NOT SIN

How can we sin in anger? We can respond with hurtful words or actions. How can we not sin in our anger? By responding with gracious words and actions. It doesn't matter what they did or said, we must respond correctly, or we have sinned against them. Am I saying there is another way to handle situations when anger is boiling over? Yes, there is. While I frequently have had to live with the consequences of handling my anger wrong, I have enjoyed the rewards when I handled it right. From personal experience: the instruction works.

In Proverbs 10:12, the scribe records Solomon said, "Hatred stirs up dissensions, but love covers over all wrongs." Anger multiplies discord but love silently covers up all sins. Solomon compares two main emotional positions and gives the normal result for each. When we repeatedly go over the events in our minds, or complain about the situation to others, we are fueling the fires of anger and hatred.

Love gives an opposite reaction: covering the offense in silence. Even in the Old Testament, a forgiving heart is described as beneficial. Proverbs 17:9 (NIV) says "He who covers over an offense promotes love, but whoever repeats the matter separates close friends." Peter gave a directive about this in 1 Peter 4:8 (NKJV): "And above all things have fervent love for one another, for love will cover a multitude of sins."

There is a word here the western mind does not comprehend. Fervent. We think passionate or intense, and those are correct – as far as they go. Those hearing Peter would know: it doesn't just mean have a passionate love. The concept is having a love that can be stretched to the breaking point, yet, it will not be broken. You might picture a strong rubber band stretched until you can pull no longer, yet without breaking. Your love can be stretched to the limit, but should not break. That is why he says, "above all things have fervent love."

Those scriptures give us a clear picture of the results of sinning in anger: discord and strife, and friendships damaged or destroyed. We also see a clear picture for "not sinning when angry": continued relationship, and silence covering the issue. Discord, or peace.

DO NOT LET THE SUN SET ON YOUR WRATH

The second phrase of Ephesians 4:26 (NIV) is: "Don't let the sun go down while you are still angry." It literally means "do not go to sleep with your anger unresolved." Normal human reaction to getting angry is to justify it. We were wronged and we need to prove it! Everyone should be just as offended by it as we are!

Why would Paul instruct us to not let the sun go down while we are angry? Doing a search on-line for the question "does short term memory become long term memory during sleep" yields a trove of scientific study reports from countries around the world. The consensus? I found everything from 'evidence points to a yes' to a firm yes. Short term memory becomes long term memory during sleep. Unresolved anger becomes resentment and bitterness in long term memory. How do we resolve the anger in our hearts, so we do not "let the sun go down on our wrath"?

Forgive! After we forgive the sin, our emotions come into line with our will choice. Our negative emotions will only be increased in strength if we do not forgive.

A FREQUENT MISAPPLICATION

A word of caution is needful here: there are those that quote "do not go to sleep with your anger unresolved" in order to force their spouse to remain awake as long as it takes to resolve the situation. This is a misapplication of the instruction from Paul. The angry spouse will be manipulating the offender to concede points or issues just so they can go to sleep. What is stated is: we are to resolve our anger before we go to sleep. We are not instructed to resolve the issue. Only our anger. Anger at being offended is resolved by forgiveness.

We can keep a clear account by forgiving as it happens, and by responding with gracious words and actions despite being angry.

That keeps a clear account of when we are hurt or offended. What about when we offend our spouse and THEY get angry? How do we handle it? We have a couple of options available to us.

THE FAILURE OPTION

The normal pattern is to act as if time heals all wounds and follow the easy route. Maybe we try to make them laugh, or distract them with a change of subject, or activity. Then we go to sleep. We have encouraged our spouse to let the sun go down on their wrath. We have avoided resolution. A delaying tactic. What occurs when we play the delay card?

We wake up the next morning and begin to talk with them, just like always. While they seem a little distant, we attribute that to anything other than the event yesterday. We could choose to blame their parent's health issues, or the restaurant didn't fix the favorite meal correctly yesterday, or the kids are having issues in school. Our spouse doesn't feel as close to us as they did before. They don't say anything, because they may not recognize their feelings have been clouded over. Since an emotional separation has begun, and neither of us recognize the cause for the change in our relationship, we continue as if nothing happened. The relationship doesn't get fixed, the separation grows. The rift and the event become elephants in the room we both ignore. "...Wide is the gate and broad is the road that leads to destruction and many enter through it. Matthew 7:13 b (NIV)" We have chosen the wide gate and the easy road that leads to destruction.

THE SUCCESS OPTION

What is the success option? "But small is the gate and narrow the road that leads to life, and only a few find it." Matthew 7:14 (NIV) The narrow way takes courage. When we know we have offended our spouse, the narrow way is to ask forgiveness. Ask forgiveness for offending. Ask forgiveness for the event. The sooner we ask, the sooner we give them an opportunity to forgive and keep a clear account.

WOUNDS WE DON'T KNOW ABOUT

While that takes care of the known situations, there is an additional exercise that will help clear the account of events we don't know about. We should ask our spouse "Have I done something I need to ask forgiveness for?" Two answers are possible: Yes or No. When we hear "yes, there is something" we have opened an opportunity to remove a blemish on our relationship account.

What if we go to our spouse every week for months and they reply, "No, there is nothing you have done to hurt or offend me." But there is. We know it. They literally refuse to bring anything up we have done or said. They are rejecting our attempts to clear the air. However, just as Paul wrote, it is still up to us to try clearing the account. Romans 12:18 (NKJV) reads: "If it is possible, as much as depends on you, live peaceably with all men."

We are responsible for our part, to go for resolution and healing. If they refuse to forgive, we will receive our healing, but they won't. We have tried to clear the account, but they may hold onto the offense, sometimes for years. Sometimes until death prevents proper face to face resolution. The reverse is true also: If they come seeking forgiveness from us, we should readily give it.

MINOR SITUATION FROM YEARS AGO

What if we go to them, and they bring up a seemingly minor situation from years ago? We sure don't want to say anything negative about the length of time it took to bring it up, or question in any way the validity of the hurt. Belittling their hurt or the delay will cause them to create a protection barrier that will take divine intervention to get past. Handle the situation the same way we do any other hurts, confess your sin to each other, and give forgiveness.

ASSIGNING BLAME

There will be times, where one or both of us will KNOW that the other is at fault. And neither of us will admit to being wrong. The situation will never be resolved if blame must be assigned.

An electronics company had invested a lot of research and development time into a new product. Prototypes were built and tested, but they didn't work properly. The facility assistant manager (we'll call him Harry) called the head of each department to a meeting to solve the problem.

Harry turned to the person on his right, and asked "what is the problem"? Billy happened to be the head of testing. He pointed to the person on his right and said, "She gave me a prototype that doesn't work." Suzy said "I built with the materials provided, according to the drawing that was made. It is design engineering's or purchasing's fault." As they went around the table, everyone pointed to the person on their right, passing the blame. It's their fault. I don't have to fix anything.

When the last person was pointed to, Jenny said: "It is all my fault. I didn't specify well enough for purchasing to buy properly. I didn't specify the concept well enough for design engineering to correctly draw the details." Jenny went all the way around the table, taking the blame for each department. After she finished taking all the blame for the failed prototypes, Harry said, "Now that blame has been assigned, let's work on fixing it." Twenty minutes later, a path to correction was developed.

A couple of months later, a new project ran into the same kind of issue. Harry called a meeting and opened it with "I didn't supervise the concept work by Jenny well enough to prevent this snafu. How do we fix it?" There was no other discussion of blame. The solution was figured out quickly.

A third project had issues. The group got together without Harry. Immediately they began working on a solution. After the meeting, Jenny went to give the solution to Harry. As she completed her report, Harry asked, "Why did you take the blame for the failure of the first project? I checked it out, your work was correct in every detail." Jenny replied, "I figured if we stopped looking to assign blame, we could start working on a solution."

The same is true in our relationships. If blame MUST be assigned, until our spouse accepts the blame, it will not be resolved. Assigning blame to others is selfish, demanding to be declared "right". It is keeping a record of wrongs. A scoreboard. For the relationship account to be cleared, we cannot require that blame be assigned, unless we take it ourselves.

Keeping a clear account is in direct opposition to society's patterns that tell us: "I am important. My rights must not be violated. Anyone who violates those rights must be punished."

Let me encourage you to learn how to respond as Paul told us; "In your anger do not sin: Do not let the sun go down while you are still angry, and do not give the devil a foothold."

The courageous among us will swallow our pride and confess when we were wrong. Confessing and seeking forgiveness requires us to be vulnerable. God expects us to choose the narrow way, and he empowers us to keep our relationship accounts clear.

Summary

KEEP A CLEAR ACCOUNT

We can choose the narrow way that leads to life, or the wide way that leads to destruction

Keeping a clear account is the courageous way.

Giving forgiveness immediately keeps a clear account.

Asking if or what we have done to offend gives opportunity for clearing the account.

Blame should not be assigned, unless we assign it to ourselves.

9

SUMMARY OF WHAT WE LEARNED

Because these principles are simple, they can be practiced by anyone, Christ follower or not. They will work, because God's instructions always work. The difficulty encountered by those who are not Christ followers, is they cannot live these concepts long term. They cannot give what they do not have. If you have not received His forgiveness, you cannot give forgiveness. If you have not received His grace, you will be unable to give grace. If you have not made Jesus Christ your personal Lord and Savior, I encourage you to turn to the appendix, review it, and follow the instructions, then come back to pick up here.

Performers in theater, music and athletics know the best way to get better at something is to practice it correctly. Music teachers are fond of saying things like "perfect practice makes perfect." Coaches remind their players they won't get it right in the game if they don't repeatedly get it right in practice. The best way to develop these concepts starts with the foundation of a relationship with Jesus Christ. Daily employ your mind by saying them out loud. Daily employ your will by committing to follow them.

Whenever I talk with someone, I give these principles in four easy to remember statements:

Live forgiveness.
Care for each other's hearts.
Give grace.

Keep a clear account.

Since each chapter is too lengthy for easy thinking about each principle every morning, allow me to give a synopsis of the concepts here. Whenever a refresher course of the details is needed, please go back and re-read the chapter that discusses the principle in detail.

In the second chapter we learned about forgiveness:

- Forgiveness is an act that we choose in spite of evidence or our emotions.
- Forgiveness can be given as early as during the event.
- If we wait until our anger or hurt goes away to forgive, we won't.
- We give up all of our rights to remain angry or hurt, or to hold the offense against them.
- We give up our rights for any kind of penalty or punishment to the offender.
- The offender should be told forgiveness was given only when they ask for it.

In the third chapter, we learned about caring for each other's hearts:

- Caring for each other's hearts is acting out God's instructions for proper relationships.
- Husbands loving their wives.
- Wives respecting their husbands.
- Thinking about our spouse instead of ourselves.

- Our instructed actions are our spouse's primary need from us.

In the fourth chapter we focused on caring for each other's hearts by our words:

- Our words affect lives for better or worse.
- Critical or condemning words are emotional poison.
- Affirming or encouraging/uplifting words are emotional fertilizer.
- Our silent thoughts about our spouse are as important as our spoken words.
- We need to increase affirmations.
- We need to end criticisms and condemnations.

In the fifth chapter, our focus shifted to our actions:

- If we say positive, encouraging things, our repeated actions should reinforce our words.
- Simple actions can mean a lot.
- Changing from a negative to a positive pattern of behavior in specific areas shows we do care about our spouses needs and desires.
- Our actions need to match our words, or our words are empty.

In the sixth chapter we learned about caring for each other's hearts by healing old emotional wounds:

- Emotional wounds can cause "over the top" negative reactions to current events.
- We can respond to make the situation worse, or to heal the wound.

- To resolve the wound we need to:
  - Resolve the immediate situation by forgiving.
  - Gently search for the root event that caused the initial wound.
  - Forgive the original offense.

In the seventh chapter we learned about giving grace:

- Because our histories are different, we think or respond differently.
- Our filters will distort our understanding of what our spouse is saying or doing.
- We should bear with and keep silent to others about the negatives of our spouse. (I am not talking about abuse here!)
- We should eagerly anticipate and expect our spouse to act with our best interests in mind.
- We should act with our spouses best interests in mind.
- We should seek out ways to work together for understanding and resolution.

In the eighth chapter we learned about keeping a clear account,

- We can choose the narrow way that leads to life, or the wide way that leads to destruction
- Keeping a clear account is the courageous way.
- Giving forgiveness immediately keeps a clear account.
- Asking if or what we have done to offend gives opportunity for clearing the account.

Summary Of What We Learned

- Blame should not be assigned, unless we assign it to ourselves.

These concepts are how my wife Anita and I are growing more in love and intimacy with each other every day. These concepts work, but only as we work them out. My prayer is for you to reap the rewards of following God's relationship principles. May Almighty God give you peace, happiness and joy inexpressible as your marriage is transformed into the intimate and fulfilling relationship He designed it to be.

APPENDIX A

We have all learned to live by our wits. Developed coping methods to deal with pain. Created defensive maneuvers to protect ourselves from emotional attacks. Employing those actions and following our own moral standards is living apart from God. God calls that sin. He also says that if we acknowledge Him in all our ways, He will direct our paths.

To be able to acknowledge Him in all our ways, He must be first in our life.

For Him to be first in our life, He must be in our life.

If you want Him in your life, tell Him, saying it out loud. Tell Him your life is messed up, that you don't have any solutions, that you need help. He wants to give you real life, God life; He wants to be your life. Confess your failure, your sin, your self-centeredness. Ask Him to forgive you. Invite Him to be the leader of your life, to be your Savior and Lord. Commit to following Him all the days of your life.

BIBLIOGRAPHY

Strong's Concordance

Biblesoft's New Exhaustive Strong's Numbers and Concordance with Expanded Greek-Hebrew Dictionary. Copyright © 1994, 2003, 2006, 2010 Biblesoft, Inc. and International Bible Translators, Inc.

Scripture references taken from:

NKJV 2007

NIV 1991

NASB 1995

www.ingramcontent.com/pod-product-compliance
Ingram Content Group UK Ltd.
Pitfield, Milton Keynes, MK11 3LW, UK
UKHW041954230426
12048UKWH00008B/332